Mitchell Levy on Creating Thought Leaders (2nd Edition)

Helping Experts Inside Corporations Amplify
Their Thought Leadership

By Mitchell Levy

Foreword by Marshall Goldsmith
Afterword by Jeffrey Hayzlett

An Actionable Business Journal

E-mail: info@thinkaha.com
20660 Stevens Creek Blvd., Suite 210
Cupertino, CA 95014

Published by THiNKaha®
20660 Stevens Creek Blvd., Suite 210, Cupertino, CA 95014
http://thinkaha.com
E-mail: info@thinkaha.com

Second Edition: March 2016
First Edition: May 2013
Paperback ISBN (Second Edition): 978-1-61699-182-1 (1-61699-182-8)
eBook ISBN (Second Edition): 978-1-61699-183-8 (1-61699-183-6)
Paperback (First Edition): 978-1-61699-118-0 (1-61699-118-6)
eBook ISBN (First Edition): 978-1-61699-119-7 (1-61699-119-4)
Place of Publication: Silicon Valley, California, USA
Library of Congress Number: 2016902846

Trademarks

All terms mentioned in this book that are known to be trademarks or service marks have been appropriately capitalized. Neither THiNKaha, nor any of its imprints, can attest to the accuracy of this information. Use of a term in this book should not be regarded as affecting the validity of any trademark or service mark.

Warning and Disclaimer

Every effort has been made to make this book as complete and as accurate as possible. The information provided is on an "as is" basis. The author(s), publisher, and their agents assume no responsibility for errors or omissions. Nor do they assume liability or responsibility to any person or entity with respect to any loss or damages arising from the use of information contained herein.

Advance Praise

"No matter what your business is, thought leadership drives customer awareness, brand loyalty, and long-term profitability. Mitchell has captured the 'secret sauce' of what it takes to be a thought leader. Read this book NOW, whether you are in a large corporation or are an entrepreneur. It will increase your value overnight!"

Thomas White, President, C-Suite Holdings, LLC | CEO Network

"Bookstores, including online stores, carry titles galore on the topic of leadership. In this book, Mitchell has carefully extracted age-old wisdom from many sources and made it easy to grasp and follow by anyone wanting to succeed as a thought leader. I especially like his H.E.L.P. prescription for leaders!"

Vish Mishra, Venture Director, Clearstone Venture Partners

"This book does a great job of driving home the point that anyone can rise to the top of their field and become the well-known expert thought leader!"

Gino Blefari, Founder, President & CEO, Intero Real Estate Services Inc.

"This book fills a need that many companies don't serve well—helping internal subject-matter experts become industry thought leaders!"

Rick Miller, President & CEO, Choices & Success

"There's an old saying that a person can't be a prophet in his or her own land. But accomplishing anything great in an organization requires being perceived as credible by those we hope to influence. It's great to have a guru like Mitchell chart a course that each of us can follow to establish that credibility and become thought leaders in our own lands so we can all get more great things done."

Ted Cocheu, Founder, Altus365

"If Twitter is the forum for short and concise thoughts and comments, then this THiNKaha book on creating thought leaders is the short and concise resource to becoming known for your expertise. Take just a few moments to read through this book and you'll quickly be on the way to being recognized as a thought leader inside and outside of your organization."

Shep Hyken, *New York Times* Bestselling Author of *The Amazement Revolution*

"Mitchell and his creative company at THiNKaha have been enlightening and so helpful in educating myself and my company in how to get my message to the world. Mitchell takes on a hands-on approach that is very comforting. His knowledge in this space is very unique and the integrity in which he works is noteworthy. I will continue to work with Mitchell in the years to come."

Greg Herlean, Founder, Horizon Trust Company

"In a world that cries out for rich content, Mitchell's book carves the meat for you in easy-to-digest portions that will help you earn the modern currency for today's corporate and personal brand development."

Willis Turner, CAE, CME, CSE (@willisturner), President & CEO, Sales & Marketing Executives International, Inc. (SMEIWorldwide)

"We need more thought leaders, and fewer thought followers. If you want to change the world, you can't follow someone else's recipe. You need to push the boundaries of conventional wisdom. You need to be a thought leader."

Bill Reichert, Managing Director, Garage Technology Ventures

"Thought leaders (not thought followers) are those that will challenge the legacy, define the current, and lead the next. Mitchell's writings takes one through the evolution of why thought leaders—and not thought followers—are so important to our advancement in everything we do and lead."

C. Finnegan Faldi, President & CEO, TruEffect, Inc.

"Fresh, straightforward, and an easy approach to inspiring corporate thought leadership that is critical to innovation and revenue growth. Mitchell does it again. This book is a must-have thought-leadership tool for corporations inspiring to be nimble and grow market share."

Carol Anderson Smith, Former HP Executive, CEO, Revenue Attraction

"Mitchell has produced a book of tremendous value to experts who want to become thought leaders. Thought leadership is increasingly necessary in our era where we are constantly inundated by media and it is necessary to find and distinguish valuable insights from experienced leaders. This book provides concise and useful tools for the practice of thought leadership."

Kyung H. Yoon, CEO, Talent Age Associates LLC

"Although people might ALREADY Know How to Be a GREAT thought leader, most are not recognized as such. Mitchell's book will help you identify and remove the interference that's holding you back from becoming the well-known recognized thought leader that you are."

Alan Fine, World-Renowned Performance Expert, *New York Times* Bestselling Author of *You ALREADY Know How to Be GREAT*

"In a world where getting the word out is key and knowledge is a currency, Mitchell's book is the ticket!"

Jacques Bazinet, VP of Corporate Development, InsideOut Development

"In the brick-and-mortar world of the last century, our ability to meet in person over time created trust to do business together. In today's virtual world, where we often can't be seen, being able to connect with people across time zones and geographies begs that we quickly demonstrate our possession of 'thought leadership' to build trust. Mitchell's latest book is spot on with dozens of ideas for helping known and unknown experts punch up their weight and be heard as the trusted advisor who can help solve people's challenges."

Mike Agron, Co-founder & Executive Webinar Producer, WebAttract

"If you are an expert, here is how to get known for it! Trusted experts will reach more people and make a greater impact by using this actionable business summary."

David Horsager, International Speaker, Bestselling Author of *The Trust Edge*

"Part of being a genius is turning a seemingly complicated situation into an easy-to-understand, step-by-step process. Mitchell is a genius at marketing. He has a simple, yet seldom used, process to position you as a leader in your field. As a thought leader/expert, you will sell more and become the trusted authority in your marketplace."

Barry Spilchuk, Author, *THE CANCER DANCE,* Co-author, *A Cup of Chicken Soup for the Soul*®

"As Mitchell exclaims in AhaMessage #13: 'Becoming a thought leader is no longer a mere luxury or pie-in-the-sky pipe dream. It's a necessity in today's world.' This THiNKaha book is a brilliant manifesto in a simple platform (a hallmark of a great thought leader) and is a must-read for industry experts looking to take their career, personal brand, and company to the next level."

Loren McDonald, VP of Industry Relations, Silverpop

Dedication

As this is my eighteenth book (now forty-six books written), I've written many dedications, and most of them have been to my wife and son. This one is no exception. I can do what I do because of the love and support of my family. I want to single out my wife, who has truly helped me be a better human being. Thank you!

Acknowledgments

Almost everything I have done in my career has helped me get to where I am now. The ability to help people succeed by putting tools in their hands has been a mantra of mine since the '90s. I want to acknowledge everyone I've intereacted with who has helped shape who I am and what I do, whether it was those who went to the conferences I ran, the university educational programs I set up, the classes I taught, those at corporations I've coached strategically, the countless CEOs I've mentored, or the numerous 1x1 coaching clients. Even today as I'm once again morphing into a new persona, I have a wealth of folks I want to thank, including Jeffrey Hayzlett's mastermind group, Bill Shepard's CEO group, my CXO networking group, and a large number of my executive editors and authors whom I've bounced the ideas contained in this book off of. Thank you!

Why I Wrote This Book

I've been creating thought leaders inside of corporations since I worked at Sun Microsystems in the '90s and as an e-commerce thought leader from 1997 to 2005 and a publisher since 2005. There is nothing more exciting than helping someone craft their message in a way in which their prospects will pay attention. The rate at which the world is changing with the existing platforms that are being dreamt of and implemented on a quicker and quicker timeline is dazzling. The megaphone that is in the hands of anyone who wants it is pervasive. Imagine going to lunch on a street with twenty-five restaurants, and every restaurant has an active karaoke session. How do you choose what to do and where to go?

Having published over a couple hundred books; booked over one thousand speakers at conferences, academic institutions, and networking events; and blogged and written hundreds of articles, there's something I do well: I know how to curate content. Curating content (i.e., you don't have to write it all yourself) is what the twenty-first century thought leader is all about. I want more people to know that. I want more people to do that. I want more people to succeed. Most of all, I want more people to get H.E.L.P. (see Section VII).

Mitchell Levy

Chief Instigator of Ahas at THiNKaha®
mitchell.levy@thinkaha.com
@happyabout
@thinkaha

How to Read a THiNKaha® Book
A Note from the Publisher

The THiNKaha series is the CliffsNotes of the 21st century. The value of these books is that they are contextual in nature. Although the actual words won't change, their meaning will change every time you read one as your context will change. Experience your own "aha!" moments ("ahas") with a THiNKaha book; ahas are looked at as "actionable" moments—think of a specific project you're working on, an event, a sales deal, a personal issue, etc. and see how the ahas in this book can inspire your own ahas, something that you can specifically act on. Here's how to read one of these books and have it work for you.

1. Read a THiNKaha book (these slim and handy books should only take about 15–20 minutes of your time!) and write down one to three actionable items you thought of while reading it. Each journal-style THiNKaha book is equipped with space for you to write down your notes and thoughts underneath each aha.

2. Mark your calendar to re-read this book again in 30 days.

3. Repeat step #1 and write down one to three more ahas that grab you this time. I guarantee that they will be different than the first time. BTW: this is also a great time to reflect on the actions taken from the last set of ahas you wrote down.

After reading a THiNKaha book, writing down your ahas, re-reading it, and writing down more ahas, you'll begin to see how these books contextually apply to you. THiNKaha books advocate for continuous, lifelong learning. They will help you transform your ahas into actionable items with tangible results until you no longer have to say "aha!" to these moments—they'll become part of your daily practice as you continue to grow and learn.

As the Chief Instigator of Ahas at THiNKaha, I definitely practice what I preach. I read *Alexisms* and *Ted Rubin on How to Look People in the Eye Digitally*, and one new book once a month and take away two to three different action items from each of them every time. Please e-mail me your ahas today!

Mitchell Levy
publisher@thinkaha.com

Contents

Foreword by Marshall Goldsmith

In line with the concept of this book, I will keep my foreword short. This is the career Bible for thought leaders! It clearly shows you how to turn your expertise into thought leadership, which is a necessary concept for successful twenty-first century organizations.

Marshall Goldsmith
The Most Influential Leadership Thinker in the World (Thinkers50 Survey—Sponsored by *Harvard Business Review*)

Introduction

Thought leadership is not something you start one day and then you are instantly recognized as a thought leader the next. If this is a new process for you, it will be a new way of life, a new way in which you conduct yourself day in and day out.

I have a couple of complementary books that I'd like to recommend to help you on your journey.

There's a book by Marsha Friedman called *Celebritize Yourself,*[1] which this book is modeled after, that discusses the concepts in this book in more detail.

There's a book in the THiNKaha series by Liz Alexander and Craig Badings that gives a great overall perspective on thought leadership and what companies need to do and think about, which is called *#THOUGHT LEADERSHIP tweet.*[2]

A couple other books in the THiNKaha series that are worth exploring are *#CROWDSOURCING tweet*[3] by Kiruba Shankar and myself and *#MY BRAND tweet*[4] by Laura Lowell.

1. Marsha Friedman, *Celebritize Yourself: The Three Step Method to Increase Your Visibility and Explode Your Business* (Warren Publishing, 2009).
2. Liz Alexander, PhD, and Craig Badings, *#THOUGHT LEADERSHIP tweet Book01: 140 Prompts for Designing and Executing an Effective Thought Leadership Campaign* (Cupertino, CA: THiNKaha, 2012).
3. Kiruba Shankar and Mitchell Levy, *#CROWDSOURCING tweet Book01: 140 Bite-Sized Ideas to Leverage the Wisdom of the Crowd* (Cupertino, CA: THiNKaha, 2011).
4. Laura Lowell, *#MY BRAND tweet Book01: Everything You Need to Know about Personal Branding in 140 Characters or Less* (Cupertino, CA: THiNKaha, 2011).

Section I: Why Should You Be a Thought Leader?

Section 1

Why Should You Be a Thought Leader?

In this first section, I define the terms *expert,*
thought leader, and *guru* and describe why it
might make sense for you to be recognized
in your field for what you do.

1

An expert has knowledge in a key area. A thought leader is a recognized expert (go-to person) in their space. @happyabout

_____

_____

_____

2

Do you have expertise in your field? Are you the go-to person for the subject matter you are an expert in? @happyabout

_____

_____

_____

3

Becoming well-known and respected for your knowledge is what being a thought leader is all about. @happyabout

_____

_____

_____

4

Thought leaders are typically experts inside a company, while gurus are experts outside corporate walls. @happyabout

_____

_____

_____

5

Organizations need to create and nurture their experts - thought leaders - if they want to keep them employed. @happyabout

_____

_____

_____

6

If you're not a thought leader in your field, someone else will be, so step in and start becoming one today! @happyabout

_____

_____

_____

7

How big is your market? Defining your market finitely enough allows you to be a thought leader in it. @happyabout

_____

_____

_____

8

The key benefit of being a thought leader is that future advocates will seek out your expertise and help. @happyabout

_____

_____

_____

9

Do you genuinely care and continuously demonstrate a strong, innate purpose to help others? If not, you need to! @happyabout

_____

_____

_____

10

The thought leader you want to be is one who wants to share knowledge and help people be more successful. @happyabout

_____

_____

_____

11

The world seeks brands. People listen to and buy from people they know, like, and trust. @happyabout

_____

_____

_____

12

Being a thought leader has tremendous benefits to your self-esteem, business, and finances. @happyabout

_____

_____

_____

13

Becoming a thought leader is no longer a mere luxury or pie-in-the-sky pipe dream. It's a necessity in today's world. @happyabout

_____

_____

_____

14

In our media-saturated world, being a thought leader is nothing less than a prerequisite for success. @happyabout

_____

_____

_____

15

Being a thought leader opens doors. People listen to you and thank you for sharing your vision. @happyabout

_____

_____

_____

Section II

What Does It Take to Be a Thought Leader?

What attributes are typically seen in thought leaders? What activities should you be focused on? Where should you be sharing your wisdom?

16

Being a thought leader means different things to different people - what does it mean to you? @happyabout

_____

_____

_____

17

Step 1 to becoming a thought leader: you want to be one! @happyabout

_____

_____

_____

18

Step 2 to becoming a thought leader: write a book about the topic you are an expert in! @happyabout

_____

_____

_____

19

To be a thought leader, you must recognize that your knowledge and expertise is valued by others. @happyabout

_____

_____

_____

20

To be a thought leader, you need to think of yourself as one. How you perceive yourself helps to create the reality. @happyabout

_____

_____

_____

21

To be a thought leader, you need to act on your dreams, go after what you want, and make it happen. @happyabout

_____

_____

_____

22

To be a thought leader, you need talent, hard work, perseverance, luck, street smarts, research, and to take action. @happyabout

_____

_____

_____

23

To be a thought leader, don't wait for the opportunity to hit you in the face. Create it! @happyabout

_____

_____

_____

24

Anyone can rise to the top of their field and become a well-known thought leader - the go-to person - in their industry. @happyabout

_____

_____

_____

25

To start on your path to thought leadership, write down your top five strengths and your top five weaknesses. @happyabout

_____

_____

_____

26

A weakness is not a fault. If you work on fixing and improving a weakness, it could turn into a strength. @happyabout

_____

_____

_____

27

Being a thought leader is typically a team effort with much behind-the-scenes support. @happyabout

_____

_____

_____

28

Thought leaders (TL) benefit with or without org support; orgs benefit when they truly embrace and support its TLs. @happyabout

_____

_____

_____

29

Part of the process of being a thought leader is sharing your expertise, and talking about you and what you can do. @happyabout

_____

_____

_____

30

Successful thought leaders have messages they are enthusiastic about & state why they are the ones to communicate it. @happyabout

_____

_____

_____

31

Successful thought leaders know who they are communicating to and how their message will help them. @happyabout

_____

_____

_____

32

Know how others have communicated
your points in the past and how
you are communicating them
differently. @happyabout

_____

_____

_____

33

See yourself as a thought leader and so too
will others! @happyabout

_____

_____

_____

Section III

Who Has Made the Transition to Thought Leader/Guru?

This section contains examples of individuals who made their way from expert to thought leader.

34

Marc Benioff started Salesforce in '99 in a rented apartment and became a thought leader/visionary/champion of SaaS. @happyabout

_____

_____

_____

35

Geoffrey Moore become well-known after spending six figures to market and push his book, "Crossing the Chasm". @happyabout

_____

_____

_____

36

Tim Ferriss was working as a sales exec as he penned his blockbuster best-seller, "The 4-Hour Workweek". @happyabout

_____

_____

_____

37

Jeffrey Hayzlett was at Kodak when he penned his 1st book, and used that to draw attention to both Kodak and himself.
@happyabout

38

Tim Sanders was with Mark Cuban and then with Yahoo! as he built his platform to become the thought leader he is today.
@happyabout

39

Vineet Nayar wrote "Employees First, Customers Second" while he served as HCL's CEO, to win personally & professionally. @happyabout

_____

_____

_____

40

Chip Conley wrote bestsellers while serving as CEO of Joie de Vivre hotels before transitioning to a thought leader. @happyabout

_____

_____

_____

41

John Chambers used his corporate platform to create a thought leader vision that helped reshape the tech industry. @happyabout

_____

_____

_____

42

Booz & Company created the Innovation 1000, which positions them as the go-to company orgs can use to be innovative. @happyabout

_____

_____

_____

43

Guy Kawasaki is one of the best known non-CEO thought leaders in the world who started out as an evangelist at Apple. @happyabout

_____

_____

_____

44

Steve Jobs is the best known thought leader/influencer of the twenty-first century. He completely changed our world! @happyabout

_____

_____

_____

Section IV

Benefits of Being a Thought Leader

So if you make the journey from expert to thought leader, is it worth it? How are you viewed? What does it mean? Where do you go from there?

45

Before you start on the thought leadership path, write down the five reasons why you want to be one in your field. @happyabout

_____

_____

_____

46

Often, very little changes from one's pre-thought-leader days other than the perception of those who now meet them. @happyabout

_____

_____

_____

47

Thought leaders are known; they are recognized. Rightly or wrongly, they are more trusted. @happyabout

_____

_____

_____

48

When thought leaders speak, people listen! It's one of life's few remaining truisms. @happyabout

_____

_____

_____

49

Thought leaders' words and actions will change people's lives. Create messages that bring about good. @happyabout

_____

_____

_____

50

Thought leaders take on many roles, all important: author, media personality, advocate, industry spokesperson, etc. @happyabout

_____

_____

_____

51

Thought leaders are asked to speak at events, endorse books, & participate in joint marketing activities. @happyabout

_____

_____

_____

52

Inside your org, thought leaders will be asked for their opinion and are expected to lead relevant meetings. @happyabout

_____

_____

_____

53

Thought leader status brings you access to key events, an identity, credibility, and buy-in. @happyabout

_____

_____

_____

54

Prospects making purchasing decisions look for thought leaders in their space to learn from before taking action. @happyabout

_____

_____

_____

55

Thought leaders create trends and influence the industry. @happyabout

_____

_____

_____

Section V

Defining Your Space and Creating Your Opportunity

What are you a thought leader in? Who are the other thought leaders occupying this space? What do you need to do to create your own space and opportunity within it?

56

Are you a thought leader? What are you an expert in, and who knows about it? @happyabout

_____

_____

_____

57

The more focused you can define your thought leader space, the easier it will be for you to reach your audience. @happyabout

_____

_____

_____

58

Thought leader questions: Who is your audience? Is it narrowly or widely defined? How can you reach them? @happyabout

_____

_____

_____

59

As a thought leader, write down 5 things you'd like to change about your space. What stands out as easy to influence? @happyabout

_____

_____

_____

60

Are there trends going in the wrong direction? Are there different ways to do the same thing? Be the thought leader. @happyabout

_____

_____

_____

61

You are on the right path when you believe your knowledge is valuable to others and have the passion to share it. @happyabout

_____

_____

_____

62

Thought leaders need to find the message that will resonate with their audience - the one that will inspire action. @happyabout

_____

_____

_____

63

Unleash your desire! Pick the cause that you have passion about, and create the messages that will resonate with your audience. @happyabout

_____

_____

_____

64

Your unique messaging, revolutionary platform, and passion about the topic will carry you to the next level. @happyabout

_____

_____

_____

65

You will change. Time will march on. The you of tomorrow is not the you of yesterday, and you need to morph over time. @happyabout

_____

_____

_____

66

Make sure that your message is not too constrained by your corporate culture and adversity to risk. @happyabout

_____

_____

_____

67

If you find a great message worth building a thought leader around, but it's not you, find the person to run with it. @happyabout

_____

_____

_____

68

Those who make it as thought leaders don't just want it; they are passionate and driven to make it happen. @happyabout

_____

_____

_____

69

Do you need to be bigger, tougher, louder, stronger, wiser? You don't need it all, but you must be distinctive. @happyabout

_____

_____

_____

70

Carefully rehearse, analyze, refocus, and rehearse your thought leader messages again and again. @happyabout

_____

_____

_____

71

Thought leaders need to write, write, write. Blogs, tweets, articles, etc. are great; books are better. @happyabout

_____

_____

_____

72

As much as you build your message around a theme, you must revolve your book around your unique and worthy message. @happyabout

_____

_____

_____

73

Writing a book is not as hard and daunting as you think. It could take 2-6 hrs to write a social media enabled AhaBook. @happyabout

_____

_____

_____

74

Thought leaders need a series of eBooks or online and physical AhaBooks and to manage an AhaLibrary tailored to their messages and vertical markets. @happyabout

_____

_____

_____

75

In broad terms, thought leadership is about making a meaningful promise and living up to it. @happyabout

_____

_____

_____

76

There is one reason thought leaders make it look so easy: they work at it all day, every day. @happyabout

_____

_____

_____

Section VI

Craft and Refine Your Message

What should you say? Why do people want to listen? How are you going to create action from your audience?

77

Take your unique thought leadership message and see how it helps accomplish both your and your org's goals. @happyabout

_____

_____

_____

78

Your thought leadership message should be easy to articulate & remember - each element of it fostering an action. @happyabout

_____

_____

_____

79

Test drive your thought leadership messaging. Does it appeal to others - both inside and outside the org? @happyabout

---

80

The target audience of your thought leadership message should be the prospects for your business or their influencers. @happyabout

---

81

Make your book your thought leadership message! @happyabout

_____

_____

_____

82

Is your message reflected on your org's website and thought leadership pieces? @happyabout

_____

_____

_____

83

Can your thought leadership messages be easily communicated with social media? @happyabout

_____

_____

_____

84

What is your thought leadership goal? With your goal in mind, every move you make should help you reach it. @happyabout

_____

_____

_____

Section VII

Thought Leaders Need H.E.L.P.

In order to transform from expert to thought leader, you need to get H.E.L.P. This acronym (which stands for **H**ealthy Following, **E**xecution, **L**eadership, and **P**roven Platform) spells out the components you need to focus on to be successful.

85

The acronym H.E.L.P. is easy to remember and articulate. Review your thought leadership progress on achieving it monthly. @happyabout

_____

_____

86

H of H.E.L.P. is for Healthy Following - who knows about you and wants to know what you have to say? @happyabout

_____

_____

87

There are people inside of your org who know and respect your thought leadership. How about people outside the org?
@happyabout

_____

_____

_____

88

What's the right social media platform(s) for you to build your following? LinkedIn, Twitter, Facebook, blog sites, etc.
@happyabout

_____

_____

_____

89

E of H.E.L.P. is for Execution. Every time you perform a task or interact with someone, you need to execute well. @happyabout

_____

_____

_____

90

Do you deliver your thought leadership promises on time and on budget? If not, how can you fix that? @happyabout

_____

_____

_____

91

Your thought leadership brand is represented in how you treat others and their experiences in interacting with you. @happyabout

_____

_____

_____

92

L of H.E.L.P. is for Leadership. Continually share leadership pieces with existing followers while building new ones. @happyabout

_____

_____

_____

93

Continuity and repetition of your thought leadership message in your market is important. @happyabout

---

94

Note that a 250-word blog post or a 140-character tweet can be thought leadership. @happyabout

---

95

P of H.E.L.P. is for Proven Platform, which is how you reach your existing followers and build new ones. @happyabout

_____

_____

_____

96

Working in a large org guarantees a large built-in thought leadership platform.
One e-mail or IM can reach a large audience.
@happyabout

_____

_____

_____

97

A benefit of the internal "organizations" platform is that you are respected and have instant credibility. @happyabout

---

98

Test drive your messages and approach on your existing platform, then use that platform to expand to others. @happyabout

---

99

Successful thought leaders run continuous campaigns to build their following on both their and other people's platforms. @happyabout

_____

_____

_____

100

Have you picked the right thought leadership teammates? Those who want to help you succeed and share common goals? @happyabout

_____

_____

_____

101

Is the org committed to using its resources to build your following and enhance your thought leadership? @happyabout

Section VIII

Tips to Start on the Thought Leader Path Today

You just want to get started. Here are a number of tips. The first is your book. You need a book specifically on the topic you want to be a thought leader in. Next, you need to spread the word about it.

Note: This book is the culmination of over eighteen years of work. That said, its creation is the foundation of my platform as thought leader creator.

102

The 3-step Marsha Friedman Celebritize Yourself method is (1) write! (2) speak! (3) sell! @happyabout

_____

_____

_____

103

The 3-step Mitchell Levy method is (1) define your market, (2) befriend peers in the field, (3) obtain H.E.L.P. @happyabout

_____

_____

_____

104

Find partners to H.E.L.P. - coauthors, co-presenters, orgs with a platform that want to communicate your message, etc. @happyabout

_____

_____

_____

105

Make friends with other thought leaders in the space. Retweet their tweets, comment on their blogs, do them favors. @happyabout

_____

_____

_____

106

Books reach one person at a time; media appearances or speaking gigs can reach hundreds, thousands, or perhaps millions. @happyabout

_____

_____

_____

107

The reason why books are great is that anything written is perceived as truth. What's your thought leadership truth?
@happyabout

_____

_____

_____

108

Write informative articles with your byline pointing back to the thought leadership you want conveyed in the marketplace. @happyabout

_____

_____

_____

109

Find websites, newsletters, and magazines that act as consolidators for the area you are expert in. Stay up to speed.
@happyabout

110

Don't miss your opportunity because you're waiting to get started or to find that perfect moment. That moment is now!
@happyabout

Section IX

Be a Great Radio or TV Guest and Be Quoted in the News

You need to choose the medium that's good for your style and your message. What do you need to do to be successful? What should you focus on?

111

If you are an interesting media guest, people will listen and producers will invite you back. @happyabout

_____

_____

_____

112

If you have a thought leadership message, editors will answer the phone. @happyabout

_____

_____

_____

113

If your thought leadership article is good, newspapers, periodicals, and websites will publish it. @happyabout

_____

_____

_____

114

The media guest talent pool continually needs to be replenished. Do a good job and you'll be invited back. @happyabout

_____

_____

_____

115

Fame & fortune won't appear from a single event; it's continual time and energy spent that counts. @happyabout

_____

_____

_____

116

Once you publish your book, you are no longer just a civilian; you are an author. @happyabout

_____

_____

_____

117

Your book is no longer just a book;
it is your thought leadership
marketing tool. @happyabout

118

The same rules in professional speaking
don't apply to appearing as a guest on
radio and TV. @happyabout

119

As a media guest, you must learn to speak in sound bites, never exceeding ninety seconds. @happyabout

_____

_____

_____

120

The key to becoming a good guest or interviewee is to be entertaining, informative, and motivating. @happyabout

_____

_____

_____

121

Talk to your audience as you would to your coworkers, family, and friends. @happyabout

---

122

The host does not care about you achieving your goals, they care about their ratings. @happyabout

---

123

Before you speak with the media or on
a stage, do a Google search to get up to
speed on current events. @happyabout

_____

_____

_____

124

Be enthusiastic and positive no matter
what time of day it is and no matter who
you are talking to. @happyabout

_____

_____

_____

125

Your enthusiasm is contagious. Your excitement about your message radiates to the audience. @happyabout

_____

_____

_____

126

Successful thought leaders smile when they are on the air. Smiling gives their voice a more attractive tone. @happyabout

_____

_____

_____

127

You are the cheerleader for your thought leadership message. @happyabout

_____

_____

_____

128

Successful thought leaders end their media interviews with a call to action. @happyabout

_____

_____

_____

129

When you share your thought leadership message, make sure it applies directly to the audience listening to it.
@happyabout

Section X

What Else Should You Be Doing or Thinking About?

There are so many activities that you should be doing on a daily, weekly, and monthly basis. You should also consider experimenting with one to two new ideas each month (or quarter, depending on the magnitude of the idea) as the marketplace keeps changing, and you need to change with it.

130

Put the title "Author" on your business card. At least 20 percent of the people who see it will ask you about it. @happyabout

_____

_____

_____

131

How do you measure success? Have a plan; measure your results. Share your expectations and results with others. @happyabout

_____

_____

_____

132

Your commitment, desire, & discipline to achieve thought leader status must be exceeded by your actions to sustain it.
@happyabout

_____

_____

_____

133

Stay current in your field and integrate your thought leadership messages into current news. @happyabout

_____

_____

_____

134

Make a section of your org's website ground zero for your thought leadership status. @happyabout

_____

_____

_____

135

Consider creating a top tens trends in your space, or a quarterly outlook if the content changes that often. @happyabout

_____

_____

_____

136

Create stories for the media - not about you or your product - but stories that appeal to the media outlet's audience. @happyabout

_____

_____

_____

137

Send letters to the opinion editor of key newspapers. If it runs, it will continue to foster your thought leadership. @happyabout

_____

_____

_____

138

Keep your website fresh with items about you: news stories, articles, books authored, speaking engagements, etc. @happyabout

_____

_____

_____

139

Consider running your own radio, TV, or print channel. Depending on your platform, it could be very successful. @happyabout

_____

_____

_____

140

Being a thought leader is one of the most rewarding positions in life. Why not work to make it yours? @happyabout

_____

_____

_____

Appendix A: Thought Leaders Need H.E.L.P. (Summary)

I wanted to repeat the core element of Section VII here. In order to transform from expert to thought leader, you need to get H.E.L.P. This acronym (which stands for **H**ealthy Following, **E**xecution, **L**eadership, and **P**roven Platform) spells out the components you need to focus on to be successful.

Aha #85: The acronym H.E.L.P. is easy to remember and articulate. Review your progress on achieving it monthly.

Aha #86: *H* is for **H**ealthy Following—who knows about you and wants to know what you have to say?

Aha #89: *E* is for **E**xecution. Every time you perform a task or interact with someone, you need to execute well.

Aha #92: *L* is for **L**eadership. You need to continually share leadership pieces with your existing followers and build new ones.

Aha #95: *P* is for **P**roven Platform, which is how you reach your existing following and build your new one.

Appendix B: Steps to Crowdsource a THiNKaha Book

In the book *#CROWDSOURCING tweet* by Kiruba Shankar, Appendix A points to an easy way to crowdsource a book. It is repeated here. Please go to this URL for a quick and easy set of steps to crowdsource your THiNKaha book: http://thinkaha.com/write-a-book/crowdsourcing.

Afterword by Jeffrey Hayzlett

As a global businessman, I know that to be successful, you need to know what you want and then go get it. If you want to be an expert in your field, then make it happen. In this book, Mitchell hands you the reigns with the necessary tools, tips, and "aha" moments to get started. So stop thinking, jump in the saddle, and start reading.

Jeffrey Hayzlett

Global Business Celebrity, Bestselling Author, and Sometime Cowboy

About the Author

Mitchell Levy is Chief Instigator of Ahas at THiNKaha®. He and his team make it easy for corporations to easily create compelling content to help turn their experts into recognized thought leaders. Mitchell is an Amazon bestselling author with forty-six business books and a contributor at Entrepreneur Magazine, has provided strategic consulting to over one hundred companies, has advised over five hundred CEOs on critical business issues through the CEO networking groups he's run, and has been chairman of the board of a NASDAQ-listed company. Read more and connect with Mitchell at www.mitchelllevy.com.

The Aha Amplifier™ is the only thought leadership platform with a built in marketplace making it easy to share curated content from like-minded thought leaders. There are over 25k diverse AhaMessages™ from thought leaders from around the world.

The Aha Amplifier makes it easy to create, organize, and share your own thought leadership AhaMessages in digestible, bite-sized morsels. Users are able to democratize thought leadership in their organizations by: 1) Making it easy for any advocate to share existing content with their Twitter, Facebook, LinkedIn, and Google+ networks, 2) Allowing internal experts to create their own thought leadership content, and 3) Encouraging the expert's advocates to share that content on their networks.

The experience of many authors is that they have been able to create their social media enabled AhaBooks™ of 140 AhaMessages in less than a day.

Sign up for a free account at
http://www.AhaAmplifier.com today!

Please pick up a copy of this book in the Aha Amplifier and share each AhaMessage socially at
http://aha.pub/mitchelllevy.

Become a Recognized Expert in Your Field of Expertise!

Learn how **http://aha.pub/me**